BY F. SCOTT FITZGERALD

NOVELS

The Last Tycoon *(Unfinished)*
Tender Is the Night
The Great Gatsby
The Beautiful and Damned
This Side of Paradise

STORIES

Bits of Paradise
uncollected stories by F. Scott and Zelda Fitzgerald

The Pat Hobby Stories
edited and with an introduction by Arnold Gingrich

The Basil and Josephine Stories
edited and with an introduction by Jackson R. Bryer
and John Kuehl

Taps at Reveille

All the Sad Young Men

Six Tales of the Jazz Age and Other Stories
with an introduction by Frances Fitzgerald Smith

Flappers and Philosophers
with an introduction by Arthur Mizener

The Stories of F. Scott Fitzgerald
a selection of 28 stories, with an introduction
by Malcolm Cowley

Babylon Revisited and Other Stories

The Short Stories of F. Scott Fitzgerald
edited and with a preface by Matthew J. Bruccoli

I'd Die for You and Other Lost Stories
edited and with an introduction by Anne Margaret Daniel

STORIES AND ESSAYS

The Crack-Up
edited by Edmund Wilson

Afternoon of an Author
with an introduction and notes by Arthur Mizener

The Fitzgerald Reader
with an introduction by Arthur Mizener

LETTERS

F. Scott Fitzgerald: A Life in Letters
edited by Matthew J. Bruccoli

Correspondence of F. Scott Fitzgerald
edited by Matthew J. Bruccoli and Margaret M. Duggan

Letters to His Daughter
edited by Andrew Turnbull and with an introduction
by Frances Fitzgerald Lanahan

The Letters of F. Scott Fitzgerald
with an introduction by Andrew Turnbull

As Ever, Scott Fitz–: Letters Between F. Scott Fitzgerald
and His Literary Agent, Harold Ober
edited by Matthew J. Bruccoli and
Jennifer McCabe Atkinson

Dear Scott/Dear Max: The Fitzgerald-Perkins
Correspondence
edited by John Kuehl and Jackson Bryer

Dear Scott, Dearest Zelda
edited by Jackson R. Bryer and Cathy W. Barks

POEMS

Poems, 1911–1940
with an introduction by James Dickey

AND A COMEDY

The Vegetable
with an introduction by Charles Scribner III

F. SCOTT FITZGERALD
ON WRITING

Edited by LARRY W. PHILLIPS

SCRIBNER

New York   London   Toronto   Sydney   New Delhi

SCRIBNER

An Imprint of Simon & Schuster, LLC
1230 Avenue of the Americas
New York, NY 10020

This Scribner trade paperback edition November 2024

SCRIBNER and design are trademarks of Simon & Schuster, LLC

Simon & Schuster: Celebrating 100 Years of Publishing in 2024

For information about special discounts for bulk purchases, please
contact Simon & Schuster Special Sales at 1-866-506-1949 or
business@simonandschuster.com.

The Simon & Schuster Speakers Bureau can bring authors to your
live event. For more information, or to book an event, contact the
Simon & Schuster Speakers Bureau at 1-866-248-3049 or visit our
website at www.simonspeakers.com.

Interior design by Alexis Minieri

Manufactured in the United States of America

1   3   5   7   9   10   8   6   4   2

Library of Congress Cataloging-in-Publication Data has been
applied for.

ISBN 978-1-6680-7036-9
ISBN 978-1-6680-9572-0 (ebook)

For
Pam and Mary Phillips
and
Herbert Kubly

CONTENTS

Foreword   xiii
Preface   xvii

1. What a Writer Is and Does   1
2. What a Writer Is   9
3. The Act of Writing   19
4. Craft and Where It Comes From   31
5. Characters   47
6. Advice to Writers   51
7. Critics and Criticism   57
8. Fitzgerald as Critic   61
9. Publishing   67
10. The Writing Life   73

Acknowledgments   97
Source Credits   99

FOREWORD

"The history of my life is the history of the struggle between an overwhelming urge to write and a combination of circumstances bent on keeping me from it." So confessed the young Scott Fitzgerald to the readers of the *Saturday Evening Post*, in the instant flush of success over the publication of his first book, *This Side of Paradise* (1920). At the time he was jesting in earnest about his various schoolboy and college efforts to establish himself as a writer—of stories, plays, musical comedy, and poetry, much of which he eventually wove into that unabashedly autobiographical novel. Yet in hindsight, Fitzgerald's initial self-appraisal seems hauntingly prophetic of the two roller-coaster decades that followed, the enduring literary achievements punctuated by false starts, distractions, and disappointments.

Much has been written and even dramatized about the Jazz-Age personas and syncopated lives of Scott and Zelda Fitzgerald; but amidst the party lights and fireworks one prosaic fact shines

as constantly as the green light at the end of Daisy's dock: Fitzgerald was, first and last, a *writer*. His earliest aspirations were
in poetry and the theatre and, to be sure, these remained alter-
nating undercurrents throughout his life's work. But it was as
a writer of prose—of novels and short stories—that Fitzgerald
applied his poetic imagination, his dramatic vision, and his deliberate and painstaking sense of craftsmanship.

From the start Fitzgerald wanted *The Great Gatsby* to be a
"consciously artistic achievement," something "beautiful and
simple and intricately patterned." The novel and the author's
achievement speak for themselves. Yet it is revealing that he
had no qualms about discussing the elements and acts of literary creation with his editor Maxwell Perkins during the novel's
long gestation period. His voluminous correspondence with
Perkins offers a rare window into the genesis and development
of a twentieth-century classic.

Indeed, unlike Hemingway, who was usually—almost
superstitiously—reluctant to analyze the mysteries of writing,
Fitzgerald took great pleasure in offering, explaining, and ar-
guing his literary convictions. His artistry was conscious; his
craftsmanship, conscientious. And, as Larry Phillips' collec-
tion here demonstrates, Fitzgerald was characteristically unin-
hibited and generous in sharing his views. He had, in short, the
instincts of a good teacher.

Toward the end of his life Fitzgerald presided over a "College
of One" for his "beloved infidel" Sheilah Graham, to whom he
served as a devoted tutor. The detailed syllabus of literature and
history which he prepared for her reveals his profound sense

of the tradition in which he himself hoped to earn a place. Un-like Hemingway, he felt no personal rivalry with literary giants, past or present; he remained deeply involved in the world of letters and sought to communicate his ideas with fellow writers, editors, friends, and above all, his daughter, Scottie, to whom he regularly sent parental epistles on literature and life.

At the very beginning of his career Scott Fitzgerald summed up his "whole theory of writing" as follows: "An author ought to write for the youth of his own generation, the critics of the next, and the schoolmasters of ever after." Today his works are taught in virtually every high school and college across the country. How brilliantly he fulfilled—posthumously—his origi-nal goal. I can only imagine how equally pleased he would be by this opportunity to present to us his own "course" on writing.

Charles Scribner III

PREFACE

Born in 1896, F. Scott Fitzgerald came to prominence in the Jazz Age of the 1920s; his career paralleled the early decades of the century—its innocent Gibson Girl beginnings; its most glamorous and flamboyant excesses of the twenties and the Lost Generation; and the sobering thirties, darkening toward the forties and the end of his own life. In a curious way, Fitzgerald's life mirrored the decades of his nation.

Intuitively American, and of his age, Fitzgerald always had, as he once said of himself, "a more than ordinary tendency" to identify with the things outside him. And for a time, it was mutual: the country had the same tendency to identify itself with him as his reputation grew and his books sold in greater numbers.

This volume brings together the comments and observations Fitzgerald made on the subject of writing in his lifetime. It is a companion volume to the earlier *Ernest Hemingway on Writing*. Despite their separate visions, both men had a common purpose as unselfish and willing friends to other writers. Hemingway's love of instruction is well known, and, in André Le Vot's biography of Fitzgerald, he writes of Fitzgerald's "need to share what he had learned," and quotes Anthony Powell, who said that "he loved instructing. There was a schoolmasterish streak . . . an enthusiasm, simplicity of exposition, that might have offered a career as a teacher or university don." As you will discover here, Fitzgerald's advice is especially wide-ranging and various. I have tried to bring all of this together, the useful, the discouraging, and the inspirational.

We may also see in these pages the difference in beliefs on the subject of writing, between these two purely American writers. Indeed, the vision of these two authors may be emblematic of the entire American approach to viewing the world. If Hemingway's code proclaims the principle "Today is the first day of the rest of your life," Fitzgerald's was essentially the more poetic (and opposite): "Today is a day that marks an end to all the succession of days which have gone before"—a view inextricably linked and woven into time itself. Fitzgerald lived, as Malcolm Cowley wrote, as if in a "room full of clocks and calendars."

In a modern age, where the movement is always in the direction of penetrating illusion, Fitzgerald goes in the other direction, eschewing the data which would interrupt progression toward the illusion of beauty. He is one who holds each note for a long time, prolongs each chord. And now, nearing the end of the century, the chord still reverberates, in the echoes of the "yellow cocktail music" of a specifically American land.

In the twenties and the Jazz Age, it was a legend. Today, the view has shifted—perhaps in a way Fitzgerald would have appreciated. As Stephen Vincent Benét wrote, "You can take off your hats now, gentlemen, and I think perhaps you had better. This is not a legend, this is a reputation—and, seen in perspective, it may well be one of the most secure reputations of our time."

LARRY W. PHILLIPS
Monroe, Wisconsin
September 1985

F. SCOTT FITZGERALD
ON WRITING

1

What a Writer Is and Does

My whole theory of writing I can sum up in one sentence. An author ought to write for the youth of his own generation, the critics of the next, and the schoolmasters of ever after.

to the Booksellers' Convention, 1920
Letters, pp. 477–78

◆

I keep thinking of Conrad's *Nigger of the Narcissus* preface—and I believe that the important thing about a work of fiction is that the essential reaction shall be profound and enduring. And if the ending of this one [*Tender Is the Night*] is not effectual I should be gladder to think that the effect came back long afterwards, long after one had forgotten the name of the author.

to John Peale Bishop, 1934
Letters, p. 387

◆

The theory . . . I got from Conrad's preface to *The Nigger* [*of the "Narcissus"*], that the purpose of a work of fiction is to appeal to the lingering after-effects in the reader's mind as differing from, say, the purpose of oratory or philosophy which respectively leave people in a fighting or thoughtful mood.

to Ernest Hemingway, 1934
Letters, p. 336

◆

Novels are not written, or at least begun, with the idea of making an ultimate philosophical system—you tried to atone for your lack of confidence by a lack of humility before the form.

to John Peale Bishop, 1929
Letters, p. 386

◆

. . . as an author's main purpose is "to make you see," so a magazine's principal purpose is to be read.

to Max Perkins, 1934
Letters, p. 271

◆

What family resemblance there is between we three as writers is the attempt that crops up in our fiction from time to time to recapture the exact feel of a moment in time and space, exemplified by people rather than by things—that is, an attempt at what Wordsworth was trying to do rather than what Keats did with such magnificent ease, an attempt at a mature memory of a deep experience.

to Max Perkins on Hemingway,
Wolfe, and himself, 1934
Letters, p. 276

◆

Almost everything I write in novels goes, for better or worse, into the subconscious of the reader. People have told me years later things like "The Story of Benjamin Button" in the form of an anecdote, having long forgotten who wrote it. This is probably the most egotistic thing about my writing I've ever put into script or even said . . .

to Margaret Case Harriman, 1935
Letters, p. 547

◆

All good writing is *swimming under water* and holding your breath.

The Crack-Up, p. 304

◆

Whether it's something that happened twenty years ago or only yesterday, I must start out with an

emotion—one that's close to me and that I can understand.

Afternoon of an Author, p. 132

◆

Reporting the extreme things as if they were the average
things will start you on the art of fiction.

The Crack-Up, p. 178

◆

Joseph Conrad defined it more clearly, more vividly
than any man of our time:

"My task is by the power of the written word to
make you hear, to make you feel—it is, before all, to
make you see."

It's not very difficult to run back and start over
again—especially in private. What you aim at is to get
in a good race or two when the crowd is in the stand.

Afternoon of an Author, pp. 135–36

◆

"You see fiction is a trick of the mind and heart com-
posed of as many separate emotions as a magician uses
in executing a pass or a palm. When you've learned it
you forget it . . ."

"When did you learn it?"

"Oh every time I begin I have to learn it all over
again in a way. But the intangibles are down here.

Why I chose this God awful metier of sedentary days and sleepless night and endless dissatisfaction. Why I would choose it again . . .

Afternoon of an Author, p. 184

◆

The two basic stories of all times are *Cinderella* and *Jack the Giant Killer*—the charm of women and the courage of men.

The Crack-Up, p. 180

◆

The public, weary of being fooled, has gone back to its Englishmen, its memoirs and its prophets. Some of the late brilliant boys are on lecture tours . . . some are writing pot boilers, a few have definitely abandoned the literary life—they were never sufficiently aware that material, however closely observed, is as elusive as the moment in which it has its existence unless it is purified by an incorruptible style and by the catharsis of a passionate emotion.

Afternoon of an Author, p. 120

◆

There is a third article which completes the trilogy of depression [*The Crack-Up* Series]. Of course now that things seem a little brighter, or at least the intensity of that despair is fading, I can see that the writing of them was a sort of catharsis but at the time of writing them what I said seemed absolutely real. . . . I see, too, that an unfriendly critic might damn the series as the whining of a spoilt baby, but in that case so is most poetry the complaints of the eternally youthful thing that persists in the writer and merely the fact that this is prose separates it from a great many of the mutterings of Shelley, Stephen Crane and Verlaine. I am not comparing this in quality with great poems of lamentation. I am simply saying that it is not essentially different in mood.

to Julian Street, 1936
Letters, p. 553

◆

"Do you expect to be—to be—well, part of the great literary tradition?" I asked, timidly.

. . . "There's no great literary tradition . . . There's only the tradition of the eventual death of every literary tradition. The wise literary son kills his own father."

In His Own Time, pp. 162–63

◆

. . . anything is immoral that consoles, stimulates or confirms a distortion. Anything that acts in place of the natural will to live is immoral. All cheap amusement becomes, at maturity, immoral—the heroin of the soul.

In His Own Time, p. 139

◆

"That is part of the beauty of all literature. You discover that your longings are universal longings, that you're not lonely and isolated from anyone. You belong."

to Sheilah Graham, 1938
Beloved Infidel, p. 196

◆

You asked me whether I thought that in the Arts it was greater to originate a new form or to perfect it. The best answer is the one that Picasso made rather bitterly to Gertrude Stein:

"You do something first and then somebody else comes along and does it pretty."

In the opinion of any real artist the inventor, which is to say Giotto or Leonardo, is infinitely superior to the finished Tintoretto, and the original D. H. Lawrence is infinitely greater than the Steinbecks.

to Frances Scott Fitzgerald, 1940
Letters, p. 89

2

What a Writer Is

Dick doesn't necessarily see more than any one else. He merely can put down a larger proportion of what he sees.

The Beautiful and Damned, p. 20

◆

"Then you don't think the artist works from his intelligence?"

"No. He goes on improving, if he can, what he imitates in the way of style, and choosing from his own interpretation of the things around him what constitutes material. But after all every writer writes because it's his mode of living . . .

The Beautiful and Damned, p. 37

"You know I was thinking to-day that I have a great confidence in Dick. So long as he sticks to people and not to ideas, and as long as his inspirations come from life and not from art, and always granting a normal growth, I believe he'll be a big man."

"I should think the appearance of the black note-book would prove that he's going to life."

Anthony raised himself on his elbow and answered eagerly:

"He tries to go to life. So does every author except the very worst, but after all most of them live on pre-digested food. The incident or character may be from life, but the writer usually interprets it in terms of the last book he read."

The Beautiful and Damned, p. 47

◆

I never really "wrote down" until after the failure of *The Vegetable* and that was to make this book [*The Great Gatsby*] possible. I would have written down long ago if it had been profitable—I tried it unsuccessfully for the movies. People don't seem to realize that for an intelligent man writing down is about the hardest thing in the world. When people like Hughes and Stephen Whitman go wrong after one tragic book, it is because they never had any real egos or attitudes but only empty bellies and cross nerves. The bellies full and the nerves soothed with vanity they see life rosily and would be

violently insincere in writing anything but the happy
trash they do.

> to H. L. Mencken, 1925
> *Letters*, pp. 499–500

◆

. . . I avoided writers very carefully because they can per-
petuate trouble as no one else can . . .

> *The Crack-Up*, p. 73

◆

"You can pay a little money but what can you do for
meddling with a human heart? A writer's temperament is
continually making him do things he can never repair."

> *Afternoon of an Author*, p. 188

◆

There never was a good biography of a good novelist.
There couldn't be. He is too many people, if he's any
good.

> *The Crack-Up*, p. 177

◆

A writer can spin on about his adventures after thirty,
after forty, after fifty, but the criteria by which these adventures are weighed and valued are irrevocably settled
at the age of twenty-five.

> *The Crack-Up*, p. 36

◆

"There is another reason why I became an author."

"How's that?"

"Well, I used to play football in a school and there was a coach who didn't like me for a damn. Well, our school was going to play a game up on the Hudson, and I had been substituting for our climax runner who had been hurt the week before. I had a good day substituting for him so now that he was well and had taken his old place I was moved into what might be called the position of blocking back. I wasn't adapted to it, perhaps because there was less glory and less stimulation. It was cold, too, and I don't stand cold, so instead of doing my job I got thinking how grey the skies were. When the coach took me out of the game he said briefly:

" 'We simply can't depend on you.'

". . . The point is it inspired me to write a poem for the school paper which made me as big a hit with my father as if I had become a football hero. So when I went home that Christmas vacation it was in my mind that if you weren't able to function in action you might at least be able to tell about it, because you felt the same intensity—it was a back door way out of facing reality."

Afternoon of an Author, pp. 185–86

◆

From childhood I have had a daydream—what a word
for one whose entire life is spent noting them down—
about starting at scratch on a desert island and building
a comparatively high state of civilization out of the ma-
terials at hand.

Afternoon of an Author, p. 129

◆

. . . the test of a first-rate intelligence is the ability to hold
two opposed ideas in the mind at the same time, and still
retain the ability to function.

The Crack-Up, p. 69

◆

Genius goes around the world in its youth incessantly
apologizing for having large feet. What wonder that later
in life it should be inclined to raise those feet too swiftly
to fools and bores.

The Crack-Up, pp. 123–24

◆

Genius is the ability to put into effect what is in your
mind. There's no other definition of it.

The Crack-Up, p. 123

◆

To record one must be unwary.

The Crack-Up, p. 202

◆

Artistic temperament is like a king with vigor and un-limited opportunity. You shake the structure to pieces by playing with it.

The Crack-Up, p. 205

◆

I honestly think that all prize fighters, actors, writers who live by their own personal performance ought to have managers in their best years. The ephemeral part of the talent seems when it is in hiding so apart from one, so "otherwise," that it seems it ought to have some better custodian than the poor individual with whom it lodges and who is left with the bill.

to Max Perkins, 1937

Letters, p. 298

◆

The necessity of the artist in every generation has been to give his work permanence in every way by a safe shap-ing and a constant pruning, lest he be confused with the journalistic material that has attracted lesser men.

to Dayton Kohler, 1938

Letters, p. 595

◆

Someone once said—and I am quoting most inexactly—"A writer who manages to look a little more deeply into his own soul or the soul of others, finding there, through his gift, things that no other man has ever seen or dared to say, has increased the range of human life."

That is why a young writer (and I shrink at the word as much as you do) is tempted, when he comes to the crossroads of what to say and not to say as regards character and feeling, to be guided by the known, the admired and the currently accepted as he hears a voice whisper within himself, "Nobody would be interested in this feeling I have, this unimportant action—therefore it must be peculiar to me, it must not be universal nor generally interesting nor even right." But if the man's gift is deep or luck is with him, as one may choose to look at it, some other voice in that crossroads makes him write down those apparently exceptional and unimportant things and that and nothing else is his style, his personality—eventually his whole self as an artist. What he has thought to throw away or, only too often, what he *has* thrown away, was the saving grace vouchsafed him. Gertrude Stein was trying to express a similar thought when—speaking of life rather than letters—she said that we struggle against most of our exceptional qualities until we're about forty and then, too late, find out that they compose the real *us*. They were the most intimate self which we should have cherished and nourished.

Again, the above is inexact and all that I have said might lead you astray in the sense that it has led Saroyan astray and the late Tom Wolfe in imagining that writing should be a cultivation of every stray weed found in the garden. That is where talent comes in to distinguish between the standard blooms which everyone knows and are not particularly exciting, the riotous and deceitful weeds, and that tiny faint often imperceptible flower hidden in a corner which, cultivated à la Burbank, is all it will ever pay us to cultivate whether it stays small or grows to the size of an oak.

to Morton Kroll, 1939
Letters, pp. 616–17

◆

. . . the odds are against your having the type of talent that matures very quickly—most of my contemporaries did not get started at twenty-two, but usually at about twenty-seven to thirty or even later, filling in the interval with anything from journalism [or] teaching [to] sailing a tramp-schooner and going to wars. The talent that matures early is usually of the poetic [type], which mine was in large part. The prose talent depends on other factors—assimilation of material and careful selection of it, or more bluntly: having something to say and an interesting, highly developed way of saying it.

to Frances Scott Fitzgerald, 1940
Letters, p. 102

◆

Schwartz looked toward me as toward a jury.

"There's a writer for you," he said. "Knows everything and at the same time he knows nothing."

The Last Tycoon, p. 12

◆

It was my first inkling that he was a writer. And while I like writers—because if you ask a writer anything, you usually get an answer—still it belittled him in my eyes. Writers aren't people exactly. Or, if they're any good, they're a whole *lot* of people trying so hard to be one person.

The Last Tycoon, p. 12

◆

"Writers are children—even in normal times they can't keep their minds on their work."

The Last Tycoon, p. 120

◆

"It takes more than brains. You writers and artists poop out and get all mixed up, and somebody has to come in and straighten you out." He shrugged his shoulders. "You seem to take things so personally, hating people and worshipping them—always thinking people are so important—especially yourselves. You just ask to be kicked around. I like people and I like them to like me, but I wear my heart where God put it—on the inside."

The Last Tycoon, p. 17

3

The Act of Writing

"What started you writing?"

"I've written ever since I can remember. I wrote short stories in school here, I wrote plays and poetry in prep school and I wrote plays and short stories for the Triangle and the 'Lit' at Princeton. But Hugh Walpole was the man who started me writing novels. One day I picked up one of his books while riding on a train from New York to Washington. After I had read about 100 pages I thought that 'if this fellow can get away with it as an author I can too.' His books seemed to me to be as bad as possible. The principal thing he did was to make unessentials seem important, but he was one of the near-best sellers. After that I dug in and wrote my first book."

In His Own Time, pp. 250–51

◆

"You must begin by making notes. You may have to make notes for years. . . . When you think of something, when you recall something, put it where it belongs," he said. "Put it down when you think of it. You may never recapture it quite as vividly the second time."

to Sheilah Graham, 1940
Beloved Infidel, p. 239

◆

"A writer wastes nothing."

to Sheilah Graham
Beloved Infidel, p. 162

◆

While I have every hope and plan of finishing my novel [*The Great Gatsby*] in June, you know how those things often come out, and even if it takes me ten times that long I cannot let it go out unless it has the very best I'm capable of in it, or even, as I feel sometimes, something better than I'm capable of.

to Max Perkins, 1924
Letters, p. 182

◆

. . . I'm afraid I haven't quite reached the ruthless artistry which would let me cut out an exquisite bit that had no place in the context. I can cut out the almost exquisite, the adequate, even the brilliant—but a true accuracy is, as you say, still in the offing.

to John Peale Bishop, 1925
The Crack-Up, p. 271

◆

I find that revising in this case [*Tender Is the Night*] is pulling up the weaker section of the book and then the next weakest, etc.

to Max Perkins, 1934
Letters, pp. 266–67

◆

Am getting responses only from a few writers and from the movies. The novel will certain have *succès d'estime* but it may be slow in coming—alas, I may again have written a novel for novelists with little chance of its lining anybody's pockets with gold. The thing is perhaps too crowded for story readers to search it through for the story but it can't be helped, there are times when you have to get every edge of your fingernails on paper. Anyhow I think this serial publication will give it the best chance it can possibly have because it is a book that only gives its full effect on its second reading. Almost every part of it now has been revised and thought out from three to six times.

to Max Perkins on *Tender Is the Night*, 1934
Letters, pp. 264–65

◆

This is a sort of postscript to my letter of yesterday: I do think that you were doing specious reasoning in part of your letter. The fact that Ernest [Hemingway] has let himself repeat here and there a phrase would be no possible justification for my doing the same. Each of us has his virtues and one of mine happens to be a great sense of exactitude about my work. He might be able to afford a lapse in that line where I wouldn't be and after all I have got to be the final judge of what is appropriate in these cases. Max, to repeat for the third time, this is in no way a question of laziness. It is a question absolutely of self-preservation.

to Max Perkins, 1934
Letters, p. 277

◆

It has become increasingly plain to me that the very excellent organization of a long book or the finest perceptions and judgment in time of revision do not go well with liquor. A short story can be written on a bottle, but for a novel you need the mental speed that enables you to keep the whole pattern in your head and ruthlessly sacrifice the sideshows as Ernest [Hemingway] did in *A Farewell to Arms.* If a mind is slowed up ever so little it lives in the individual part of a book rather than in a book as a whole; memory is dulled. I would give anything if I hadn't had to write Part III of *Tender Is the Night* entirely on stimulant. If I had one more crack at it cold sober I believe it might have made a great difference. Even Ernest commented on sections that were needlessly included and as an artist he is as near as I know for a final reference.

to Max Perkins, 1935
Letters, p. 286

♦

. . . "You do not," he once said in understandable irritation with some of his critics, "produce a short story for the *Saturday Evening Post* on a bottle" . . .

Afternoon of an Author, p. 7

♦

Invent a system Zolaesque . . . but buy a file. On the first page of the file put down the outline of a novel of your times enormous in scale (don't worry, it will contract by itself) and work on the plan for two months. Take the central point of the file as your big climax and follow your plan backward and forward from that for another three months. Then draw up something as complicated as a continuity from what you have and set yourself a schedule.

to John O'Hara, 1936
Letters, p. 560

♦

Good stories write themselves—bad ones have to be written . . .

to Harold Ober, 1925
As Ever, Scott Fitz–, p. 76

◆

"Crack!" goes the pistol and off starts this entry. Sometimes he has caught it just right; more often he has jumped the gun. On these occasions, if he is lucky, he runs only a dozen yards, looks around and jogs sheepishly back to the starting place. But too frequently he makes the entire circuit of the track under the impression that he is leading the field, and reaches the finish to find he has no following. The race must be run all over again. . . .

So runs an interview with one of the champion false starters of the writing profession—myself. Opening a leather-bound waste-basket which I fatuously refer to as my "notebook," I pick out at random a small, triangular piece of wrapping paper with a canceled stamp on one side. On the other side is written:

Boopsie Dee was cute.

. . . There are hundreds of these hunches. Not all of them have to do with literature. Some are hunches about importing a troupe of Ouled Naïl dancers from Africa, about bringing the Grand-Guignol from Paris to New York, about resuscitating football at Princeton . . .

These little flurries caused me no travail—they were opium eaters' illusions, vanishing with the smoke of the pipe, or you know what I mean. The pleasure of thinking about them was the exact equivalent of having accomplished them. It is the six-page, ten-page, thirty-page globs of paper that grieve me professionally, like unsuccessful oil shafts; they represent my false starts.

Afternoon of an Author, pp. 127–28

◆

I am alone in the privacy of my faded blue room with my sick cat, the bare February branches waving at the window, an ironic paper weight that says Business is Good . . . and my greatest problem:

"Shall I run it out? Or shall I turn back?"

. . . Or:

"This is just bullheadedness. Better throw it away and start over."

The latter is one of the most difficult decisions that an author must make. To make it philosophically, before he has exhausted himself in a hundred-hour effort to resuscitate a corpse or disentangle innumerable wet snarls, is a test of whether or not he is really a professional. There are often occasions when such a decision is doubly difficult. In the last stages of a novel, for instance, where there is no question of junking the whole, but when an entire favorite character has to be hauled out by the heels, screeching, and dragging half a dozen good scenes with him.

It is there that these confessions tie up with a general problem as well as with those peculiar to a writer. The decision as to when to quit, as to when one is merely floundering around and causing other people trouble, has to be made frequently in a lifetime.

Afternoon of an Author, pp. 134–35

◆

"Work!" at once exclaimed Mr. Fitzgerald, his blue eyes earnest. "Work is the one salvation for all of us—even if we must work to forget there's nothing worth while to work for, even if the work we turn out—books, for example—doesn't satisfy us. The young man must work."

In His Own Time, p. 257

◆

[Upon seeing a writer pass by who was a notorious drinker:]

"There goes one of the last survivors of the 'booze and inspiration' school. Bret Harte was one of the earliest ones and it was all right in his day, but the old school of writers who learned to drink and to write while reporting for a newspaper is dying out. . . . that gang is not to be met any more. I can't think of how he [they] could have done it. For me, narcotics are deadening to work. I can understand any one drinking coffee to get a stimulating effect, but whiskey—oh, no."

"*This Side of Paradise* doesn't read as if it were written on coffee," I remarked.

"And it wasn't. You'll laugh, but it was written on coca cola. Coca cola bubbles up and fizzes inside enough to keep me awake."

In His Own Time, pp. 252–53

◆

As a matter of fact I have never written a line of any kind while I was under the glow of so much as a single cocktail and tho my parties have been many it's been their spectacularity rather than their frequency which has built up the usual "dope-fiend" story.

to Edmund Wilson, 1922

Letters, p. 355

◆

I have grown to like this particular corner of California where I shall undoubtedly stay all summer. Dates for a novel, are, as you know, uncertain, but I am blocking this out in a fashion so that, unlike *Tender* [*Is the Night*], I may be able to put it aside for a month and pick it up again at the exact spot factually and emotionally where I left off.

to Max Perkins, 1939

Letters, pp. 312–13

◆

My novel [*The Last Tycoon*] is something of a mystery, I hope. I think it's a pretty good rule not to tell what a thing is about until it's finished. If you do you always seem to lose some of it. It never quite belongs to you so much again . . .

to Frances Scott Fitzgerald, 1940
Letters, p. 117

◆

. . . sometimes you can lick an especially hard problem by facing it always the very first thing in the morning with the very freshest part of your mind. This has so often worked with me that I have an uncanny faith in it.

to Frances Scott Fitzgerald, 1940
Letters, p. 81

◆

Stories are best written in either one jump or three, according to the length. The three-jump story should be done on three successive days, then a day or so for revise and off she goes. This of course is the ideal—in many stories one strikes a snag that must be hacked at but, on the whole, stories that drag along or are terribly difficult (I mean a difficulty that comes from a poor conception and consequent faulty construction) never flow quite as well in the reading.

to Frances Scott Fitzgerald, 1940
Letters, p. 110

◆

My room is covered with charts like it used to be for *Tender Is the Night*, telling the different movements of the characters and their histories.

to Zelda Fitzgerald, 1940

Letters, p. 147

4

Craft and Where It Comes From

I hope you read a most tremendous lot, Sally—you've got a keen mind and just feed it with every bit of reading you can lay your hands on, good, poor or mediocre. A good mind has a good separator and can peck the good from the bad in all it absorbs.

to Sally Pope Taylor, 1918
Letters, p. 471

◆

Think of a romantic egotist writing about himself in a cold barracks on Sunday afternoons . . . yet that is the way this novel has been scattered into shape—for it has no form to speak of.

to Shane Leslie, 1918
Letters, p. 396

◆

My novel is autobiographical in point of view but I've borrowed incidents from all my friends' experience.

to Mrs. Edward Fitzgerald, 1919

Letters, p. 473

◆

"And so I turned, canny for my years, from the professors to the poets, listening—to the lyric tenor of Swinburne and the tenor robusto of Shelley, to Shakespeare with his first bass and his fine range, to Tennyson with his second bass and his occasional falsetto, to Milton and Marlowe, bassos profundo. I gave ear to Browning chatting, Byron declaiming, and Wordsworth droning. This, at least, did me no harm. I learned a little of beauty—enough to know that it had nothing to do with truth—and I found, moreover, that there was no great literary tradition; there was only the tradition of the eventful death of every literary tradition . . ."

The Beautiful and Damned, p. 253

◆

You ought never to use an unfamiliar word unless *you've had to* search for it to express a delicate shade—where in effect you have recreated it. This is a damn good prose rule I think. . . . Exceptions: (a) need to avoid repetition (b) need of rhythm (c) etc.

to John Peale Bishop, 1929

Letters, p. 385

◆

I was interested also in your analysis of the influences upon my own books. I never read a French author, except the usual prep-school classics, until I was twenty, but Thackeray I had read over and over by the time I was sixteen, so as far as I am concerned you guessed right.

to John Jamieson, 1934

Letters, p. 528

◆

". . . what I meant was that if big things never grip me— well, it simply means I'm not cut out to be big. This conscious struggle to find bigness outside, to substitute bigness of theme for bigness of perception, to create an objective *Magnum Opus* . . . well, all that's the antithesis of my literary aims."

In His Own Time, p. 162

◆

. . . the motif of the "dying fall" [in *Tender Is the Night*] was absolutely deliberate and did not come from any diminution of vitality but from a definite plan.

That particular trick is one that Ernest Hemingway and I worked out—probably from Conrad's preface to *The Nigger* [*of the "Narcissus"*]—and it has been the greatest "credo" in my life ever since I decided that I would rather be an artist than a careerist. I would rather impress my image (even though an image the size of a nickel) upon the soul of a people than be known except insofar as I have my natural obligation to my family—to provide for them. I would as soon be as anonymous as Rimbaud, if I could feel that I had accomplished that purpose—and that is no sentimental yapping about being disinterested. It is simply that, having once found the intensity of art, nothing else that can happen in life can ever again seem as important as the creative process.

to H. L. Mencken, 1934
Letters, p. 530

◆

[Ring Lardner] never knew anything about composition, except as it concerned the shorter forms; that is why he always needed advice from us as to how to organize his material; it was his greatest fault—the fault of many men brought up in the school of journalism—while a novelist with his sempiternal sigh can cut a few breaths. It is a hell of a lot more difficult to build up a long groan than to develop a couple of short coughs!

to Max Perkins, 1934
Letters, p. 282

◆

Years later when Ernest was writing *Farewell to Arms* he was in doubt about the ending and marketed around to

half a dozen people for their advice. I worked like hell on
the idea and only succeeded in evolving a philosophy in
his mind utterly contrary to everything that he thought
an ending should be, and [it] later convinced me that he
was right and made me end *Tender Is the Night* on a fade-
away instead of a staccato.

to John O'Hara, 1936
Letters, p. 559

◆

The point of my letter which survives is that there
were moments all through the book [*Tender Is the Night*]
where I could have pointed up dramatic scenes, and I
deliberately refrained from doing so because the material itself was so harrowing and highly charged that I
did not want to subject the reader to a series of nervous shocks in a novel that was inevitably close to
whoever read it in my generation.

Contrariwise, in dealing with figures as remote as
are a bootlegger and crook to most of us [*The Great
Gatsby*], I was not afraid of heightening and melo-
dramatizing any scenes; and I was thinking that in
your novel I would like to pass on this theory to
you for what it is worth. Such advice from fellow-
craftsmen has been a great help to me in the past,
indeed I believe it was Ernest Hemingway who developed to me, in conversation, that the dying fall
was preferable to the dramatic ending under certain

conditions, and I think we both got the germ of the idea from Conrad.

to John Peale Bishop, 1934

Letters, pp. 388–89

◆

. . . [the] care for shimmering set, active plot, bright characters, change of pace and gaiety should *all show in the plan.* Leave *out* any two, and your novel is weaker, any three or four and you're running a department store with only half the counters open.

to John Peale Bishop, 1935

Letters, pp. 393–94

◆

When you plant a scene in a book the importance of the scene cannot be taken as a measure of the space it should occupy, for it is entirely a special and particular artistic problem. If Dreiser, in *An American Tragedy*, plans to linger over the drowning in upper New York well and good, but I could tell you plenty [of] books in which the main episode, around which swings the entire drama, is over and accomplished in four or five sentences.

to John Peale Bishop, 1935

Letters, p. 391

◆

. . . I have the same *penchant* as you . . . for letting a theme *unravel* at the end, so to speak, as things do in life rather than to cut it off short, but I feel that this can be achieved without having the writing *itself* become exhausted. It is my old contention that tiredness, boredom, exhaustion, etc., must not be conveyed by the symbols which they show in life, in fact, can't be so conveyed in literature because boredom is essentially boring and tiredness is essentially tiring.

to James Boyd, 1935
Letters, p. 542

◆

I'd hate to see such an exquisite talent [as Thomas Wolfe's] turn into one of those muscle-bound and useless giants seen in a circus. Athletes have got to learn their games; they shouldn't just be content to tense their muscles, and if they do they suddenly find when called upon to bring off a necessary effect they are simply liable to hurl the shot into the crowd and not break any records at all. The metaphor is mixed but I think you will understand what I mean . . .

to Max Perkins on Thomas Wolfe, 1935
Letters, p. 289

◆

. . . the only effect I ever had on Ernest [Hemingway] was to get him in a receptive mood and say let's cut everything that goes before this. Then the pieces got mislaid and he could never find the part that I said to cut out. And so he published it without that and later we agreed that it was a very wise cut. This is not literally true and I don't want it established as part of the Hemingway legend, but it's just about as far as one writer can go in helping another.

to John O'Hara, 1936
Letters, p. 559

◆

I don't want you to give up mathematics next year. I learned about writing from doing something that I didn't have any taste for.

to Frances Scott Fitzgerald, 1936
Letters, p. 25

◆

Didn't Hemingway say this in effect: If Tom Wolfe ever learns to separate what he gets from books from what he gets from life, he will be an original. All you can get from books is rhythm and technique. He's half-grown artistically—this is truer than what Ernest said about him. But when I've criticized him (several times in talk), I've felt mad afterwards.

The Crack-Up, p. 178

◆

[My books] have alternated between being selective and blown up. *Paradise* and *Gatsby* were selective; *The Beautiful and Damned* and *Tender* aimed at being full and comprehensive—either could be cut by one-fourth, especially the former. (Of course they were cut that much but not enough.) The difference is that in these last two I wrote everything, hoping to cut to interest. In *This Side of Paradise* (in a crude way) and in *Gatsby* I selected the stuff to fit a given mood or "hauntedness" or whatever you might call it, rejecting in advance in *Gatsby*, for instance, all of the ordinary material for Long Island, big crooks, adultery theme and always starting from the *small* focal point that impressed me—my own meeting with Arnold Rothstein for instance.

to Corey Ford, 1937

Letters, p. 573

◆

About *adjectives:* all fine prose is based on the verbs carrying the sentences. They make sentences move. Probably the finest technical poem in English is Keats' "Eve of Saint Agnes." A line like "The hare limped trembling through the frozen grass," is so alive that you race through it, scarcely noticing it, yet it has colored the whole poem with its movement—the limping, trembling and freezing is going on before your own eyes.

to Frances Scott Fitzgerald, 1938

Letters, p. 43.

◆

I don't care much where I am any more, nor expect very much from places. You will understand this. To me, it is a new phase, or rather, a development of something that began long ago in my writing—to try to dig up the relevant, the essential, and especially the dramatic and glamorous from whatever life is around. I used to think that my sensory impression of the world came from outside. I used to actually believe that it was as objective as blue skies or a piece of music. Now I know it was within, and emphatically cherish what little is left.

to Gerald Murphy, 1938
Letters, p. 446

◆

The book is formless. In first novels this is permissible, perhaps even to be encouraged, as the lack of a pattern gives the young novelist more of a chance to assert his or her individuality, which is the principal thing.

In His Own Time, p. 137

◆

"By style, I mean color . . . I want to be able to do anything with words: handle slashing, flaming descriptions like Wells, and use the paradox with the clarity of Samuel Butler, the breadth of Bernard Shaw and the wit of Oscar Wilde, I want to do the wide sultry heavens of Conrad, the rolled-gold sundowns and crazy-quilt skies of Hichens and Kipling as well as the pastelle [sic] dawns and twilights of Chesterton. All that is by way of ex-

ample. As a matter of fact I am a professional literary
thief, hot after the best methods of every writer in my
generation."

In His Own Time, p. 163

♦

I'd rather have written Conrad's *Nostromo* than any
other novel. First, because I think it is the greatest novel
since *Vanity Fair* (possibly excluding *Madame Bovary*), but
chiefly because *Nostromo*, the man, intrigues me so much.
. . . I would rather have dragged his soul from behind his
astounding and inarticulate presence than written any
other novel in the world.

In His Own Time, pp. 168–69

♦

[Poetry] isn't something easy to get started on by yourself. You need, at the beginning, some enthusiast who
also knows his way around—John Peale Bishop per-
formed that office for me at Princeton. I had always
dabbled in "verse" but he made me see, in the course
of a couple of months, the difference between poetry
and non-poetry. . . .

Poetry is either something that lives like fire inside
you—like music to the musician or Marxism to the
Communist—or else it is nothing, an empty, formal-
ized bore around which pedants can endlessly drone

their notes and explanations. "The Grecian Urn" is unbearably beautiful with every syllable as inevitable as the notes in Beethoven's Ninth Symphony or it's just something you don't understand. It is what it is because an extraordinary genius paused at that point in history and touched it. I suppose I've read it a hundred times. About the tenth time I began to know what it was about, and caught the chime in it and the exquisite inner mechanics. Likewise with "The Nightingale" which I can never read through without tears in my eyes; likewise the "Pot of Basil" with its great stanzas about the two brothers, "Why were they proud, etc."; and "The Eve of St. Agnes," which has the richest, most sensuous imagery in English, not excepting Shakespeare. And finally his three or four great sonnets, "Bright Star" and the others.

Knowing those things very young and granted an ear, one could scarcely ever afterwards be unable to distinguish between gold and dross in what one read. In themselves those eight poems are a scale of workmanship for anybody who wants to know truly about words, their most utter value for evocation, persuasion or charm. For awhile after you quit Keats all other poetry seems to be only whistling or humming.

to Frances Scott Fitzgerald, 1940
Letters, pp. 105–6

◆

. . . a real grasp of Blake, Keats, etc., will bring you something you haven't dreamed of. And it should come now.

to Frances Scott Fitzgerald, 1940
Letters, p. 104

◆

Have you ever . . . read *Pere Goriot* or *Crime and Punishment* or even *A Doll's House* or *St. Matthew* or *Sons and Lovers?* A good style simply doesn't form unless you absorb half a dozen top-flight authors every year. Or rather it *forms* but, instead of being a subconscious amalgam of all that you have admired, it is simply a reflection of the last writer you have read, a watered-down journalese.

to Frances Scott Fitzgerald, 1940
Letters, pp. 102–3

◆

The chief fault in your style is its lack of distinction—something which is inclined to grow with the years. You had distinction once—there's some in your diary—and the only way to increase it is to cultivate *your own garden.* And the only thing that will help you is poetry which is the most concentrated form of style.

to Frances Scott Fitzgerald, 1940
Letters, p. 103

◆

Let me preach again for a moment: I mean that what you have felt and thought will by itself invent a new style, so that when people talk about style they are always a little astonished at the newness of it, because they think that it is only *style* that they are talking about, when what they are talking about is the attempt to express a new idea with such force that it will have the originality of the thought.

to Frances Scott Fitzgerald, 1940
The Crack-Up, p. 304

◆

The strongest should come first in comedy because once a character is really established as funny everything he does becomes funny. At least it's that way in life . . .

to Arnold Gingrich, 1940
The Pat Hobby Stories, pp. xvii–xviii

◆

So many writers, Conrad for instance, have been aided by being brought up in a métier utterly unrelated to literature. It gives an abundance of material and, more important, an attitude from which to view the world. So much writing nowadays suffers both from lack of an attitude and from sheer lack of any material, save what is accumulated in a purely social life.

The world, as a rule, does not live on beaches and in country clubs.

an undated fragment of a letter
to Frances Scott Fitzgerald
Letters, p. 121

◆

I might say that I don't think anyone can write succinct prose unless they have at least tried and failed to write a good iambic pentameter sonnet, and read Browning's short dramatic poems, etc.—but that was my personal approach to prose. Yours may be different, as Ernest Hemingway's was. But I wouldn't have written this long letter unless I distinguished, underneath the sing-song lilt of your narrative, some traces of a true rhythm . . . There is as yet no honesty—the reader will say "so what?" But when in a freak moment you will want to give the low down, not the scandal, not the merely *reported* but the *profound* essence of what happened at a prom or after it, perhaps that honesty will come to you—and then you will understand how it is possible to make even a forlorn Laplander *feel* the importance of a trip to Cartier's!

an undated fragment of a letter to
Frances Scott Fitzgerald
Letters, p. 119

5

Characters

I myself didn't know what Gatsby looked like or was engaged in and you felt it. If I'd known and kept it from you you'd have been *too impressed with my knowledge to protest.* This is a complicated idea but I'm sure you'll understand. But I know now—and as a penalty for not having known first, in other words to make sure, I'm going to tell more.

to Max Perkins, 1925

Letters, p. 193

◆

Thank you, immensely, for sending me your article. I agree with you entirely, as goes without saying, in your analysis of Gatsby. He was perhaps created on the image of some forgotten farm type of Minnesota that I have known and forgotten, and associated at the same moment with some sense of romance. It might interest you to know that a story of mine, called "Absolution," in my book *All the Sad Young Men* was intended to be a picture of his early life, but that I cut it because I preferred to preserve the sense of mystery.

to John Jamieson, 1934

Letters, p. 529

◆

In my theory, utterly opposite to Ernest's [Hemingway], about fiction, i.e., that it takes half a dozen people to make a synthesis strong enough to create a fiction character—in that theory, or rather in despite of it, I used you again and again in *Tender* [*Is the Night*]:

"Her face was hard and lovely and pitiful" and again

"He had been heavy, belly-frightened with love of her for years"

—in those and in a hundred other places I tried to evoke not *you* but the effect that you produce on men—the echoes and reverberations . . .

to Sara Murphy, 1935

Letters, p. 441

◆

Excuse me if this letter has a dogmatic ring. I have lived so long within the circle of this book and with these characters that often it seems to me that the real world does not exist but that only these characters exist, and however pretentious that remark sounds . . . it is an absolute fact—so much so that their glees and woes are just exactly as important to me as what happens in life.

to Max Perkins, 1934

Letters, p. 273

◆

Huckleberry Finn took the first journey *back*. He was the first to look *back* at the republic from the perspective of the west. His eyes were the first eyes that ever looked at us objectively that were not eyes from overseas. There were mountains at the frontier but he wanted more than mountains to look at with his restless eyes—he wanted to find out about men and how they lived together. And because he turned back we have him forever.

In His Own Time, p. 176

◆

"I had no idea of originating an American flapper when I first began to write. I simply took girls whom I knew very well and, because they interested me as unique human beings, I used them for my heroines. . . ."

In His Own Time, p. 265

◆

"Start out with an individual and you find that you have created a type—start out with a type and you find that you have created nothing."

In His Own Time, p. 480

◆

The novel is hard as pulling teeth but that is because it is in its early character-planting phase. I feel people so less intently than I did once that this is harder. It means welding together hundreds of stray impressions and incidents to form the fabric of entire personalities.

to Zelda Fitzgerald on *The Last Tycoon*, 1940
Letters, p. 149

◆

The editor of *Colliers* wants me to write for them . . . but I tell him I'm finishing my novel for myself and all I can promise him is a look at it. It will, at any rate, be nothing like anything else as I'm digging it out of myself like uranium—one ounce to the cubic ton of rejected ideas. It is a novel *à la Flaubert* without "ideas" but only people moved singly and in mass through what I hope are authentic moods.

The resemblance is rather to *Gatsby* than to anything else I've written.

to Zelda Fitzgerald, 1940
Letters, p. 151

◆

Action is character.

reference to Fitzgerald's realization of the need for action in
movie writing notes on *The Last Tycoon*, p. 163

6

Advice to Writers

Upon mature consideration I advise you to go no far-
ther with your vocabulary. If you have a lot of words
they will become like some muscle you have developed
that you are compelled to use, and you must use this
one in expressing yourself or in criticizing others. It is
hard to say who will punish you the most for this, the
dumb people who don't know what you are talking
about or the learned ones who do. But wallop you they
will and you will be forced to confine yourself to pen
and paper.

Then you will be a writer and may God have mercy
on your soul.

No! A thousand times no! Far, far better confine
yourself to a few simple expressions in life, the ones
that served billions upon countless billions of our fore-
fathers and still serve admirably all but a tiny handful
of those at present clinging to the earth's crust. . . .

So forget all that has hitherto attracted you in our complicated system of grunts and go back to those fundamental ones that have stood the test of time.

to Andrew Turnbull, 1932

Letters, pp. 517–18

♦

Great art is the contempt of a great man for small art.

The Crack-Up, p. 179

♦

You don't write because you want to say something; you write because you've got something to say.

The Crack-Up, p. 123

♦

When the first-rate author wants an exquisite heroine or a lovely morning, he finds that all the superlatives have been worn shoddy by his inferiors. It should be a rule that bad writers must start with plain heroines and ordinary mornings, and, if they are able, work up to something better.

The Crack-Up, p. 180

♦

Don't be a bit discouraged about your story not being tops. At the same time, I am not going to encourage you about it, because, after all, if you want to get into the big time, you have to have your own fences to jump and learn from experience. Nobody ever became a writer just by wanting to be one. If you have anything to say, anything you feel nobody has ever said before, you have got to feel it so desperately that you will find some way to say it that nobody has ever found before, so that the thing you have to say and the way of saying it blend as one matter—as indissolubly as if they were conceived together.

> to Frances Scott Fitzgerald, 1936
> *Letters*, p. 23

◆

There's no "Safety First" in Art.

> *In His Own Time*, p. 46

◆

If in the future your novel is published and makes a success, I should suggest that you put all rights in his hands [Harold Ober, Fitzgerald's agent]. He will charge you ten per cent, but in sixteen years of professional writing he has saved me much more than ten per cent.

> to F. B. Kerr, 1936
> *Letters*, p. 297

◆

I've read the story carefully and, Frances, I'm afraid the price for doing professional work is a good deal higher than you are prepared to pay at present. You've got to sell your heart, your strongest reactions, not the little minor things that only touch you lightly, the little experiences that you might tell at dinner. This is especially true when you *begin* to write, when you have not yet developed the tricks of interesting people on paper, when you have none of the technique which it takes time to learn. When, in short, you have *only* your emotions to sell.

This is the experience of all writers. It was necessary for Dickens to put into *Oliver Twist* the child's passionate resentment at being abused and starved that had haunted his whole childhood. Ernest Hemingway's first stories, *In Our Time*, went right down to the bottom of all that he had ever felt and known. In *This Side of Paradise* I wrote about a love affair that was still bleeding as fresh as the skin wound on a haemophile.

The amateur, seeing how the professional, having learned all that he'll ever learn about writing, can take a trivial thing such as the most superficial reactions of three uncharacterized girls and make it witty and charming—the amateur thinks he or she can do the same. But the amateur can only realize his ability to transfer his emotions to another person by some such desperate and radical expedient as tearing your first tragic love story out of your heart and putting it on pages for people to see.

That, anyhow, is the price of admission. Whether

you are prepared to pay it, or whether it coincides or conflicts with your attitude on what is "nice" is something for you to decide. But literature, even light literature, will accept nothing less from the neophyte. It is one of those professions that want the "works." You wouldn't be interested in a soldier who was only a *little* brave.

> to Frances Turnbull, a sophomore at Radcliffe, who had sent Fitzgerald one of her "Sketches by a Debutante," 1938
> *Letters*, pp. 601–2

◆

P.S. If you keep the diary, please don't let it be the dry stuff I could buy in a ten-franc guide book. I'm not interested in dates and places, even the Battle of New Orleans, unless you have some unusual reaction to them. Don't try to be witty in the writing, unless it's natural—just true and real.

> to Frances Scott Fitzgerald, 1938
> *Letters*, p. 49

◆

"When you tell an anecdote, tell it so your listeners can actually *see* the people you are talking about."

> to Sheilah Graham, 1937
> *Beloved Infidel*, p. 149

◆

While I'm on the subject, remember that Harold Ober's [Fitzgerald's agent] advice is only good up to a point. He is "the average reader" and about one third of the stories that I sold to *The Saturday Evening Post* were stories which he did not think they would buy. Like all agents, he is clogged with too much of the kind of reading trained to smell the money in the page—so I should never ask his advice on any literary matter, though of course in other regards he is an excellent agent.

to Frances Scott Fitzgerald, 1940

Letters, p. 117

♦

It is an awfully lonesome business, and, as you know, I never wanted you to go into it, but if you are going into it at all, I want you to go into it knowing the sort of things that took me years to learn.

to Frances Scott Fitzgerald, 1940

The Crack-Up, p. 304

7

Critics and Criticism

Paradise is out here. Of 20 reviews about half are mildly favorable, a quarter of them imply that I've read "*Sinister Street* [by Compton Mackenzie] once too often" and the other five (including *The Times*) damn it summarily as artificial.

to Edmund Wilson, 1921
Letters, p. 351

◆

Did you ever know a writer to calmly take a just criticism and shut up?

to H. L. Mencken, 1925
Letters, p. 499

◆

The only way I can write a decent story is to imagine no one's going to accept it and who cares. Self-consciousness about editors is *ruinous* to me. They can make their criticisms afterwards . . .

to Harold Ober, 1930
Letters, pp. 416–17

◆

There comes a time when a writer writes only for certain people and where the opinion of the others is of little less than no importance at all . . .

to Christian Gauss, 1934
Letters, p. 407

◆

In the future please send me clippings even though you do crack at me in the course of your interviews. I'd rather get them than have you send me accounts of what literary sour bellies write about me in their books. I've been criticized by experts including myself.

to Frances Scott Fitzgerald, 1940
Letters, p. 88

◆

Having been compared to Homer and Harold Bell Wright for fifteen years, I get a pretty highly developed delirium tremens at the professional reviewers: the light men who bubble at the mouth with enthusiasm because they see other bubbles floating around, the dumb men who regularly mistake your worst stuff for your best and your best for your worst, and, most of all, the cowards who straddle and the leeches who review your books in terms that they have cribbed out of the book itself, like scholars under some extraordinary dispensation which allows them to heckle the teacher. With every book I have ever published there have always been two or three people, as often as not strangers, who have seen the intention, appreciated it, and allowed me whatever percentage I rated on the achievement of that intention.

to Mabel Dodge Luhan, 1934

Letters, p. 531

♦

I'm circling closer to my theme song, which is: that I'd like to communicate to such of them who read this novel [*The Great Gatsby*] a healthy cynicism toward contemporary reviews. Without undue vanity one can permit oneself a suit of chain mail in any profession. Your pride is all you have, and if you let it be tampered with by a man who has a dozen prides to tamper with before lunch, you are promising yourself a lot of disappointments that a hard-boiled professional has learned to spare himself.

In His Own Time, pp. 155–56

♦

The genius conceives a cosmos with such transcendental force that it supersedes, in certain sensitive minds, the cosmos of which they have been previously aware. The new cosmos instantly approximates ultimate reality as closely as did the last. It is a bromide to say that the critic can only describe the force of his reaction to any specific work of art.

In His Own Time, pp. 138–39

♦

How anyone could take up the responsibility of being a novelist without a sharp and concise attitude about life is a puzzle to me. How a critic could assume a point of view which included twelve variant aspects of the social scene in a few hours seems something too dinosaurean to loom over the awful loneliness of a young author.

To circle nearer to this book [*The Great Gatsby*], one woman who could hardly have written a coherent letter in English, described it as a book that one read only as one goes to the movies around the corner. That type of criticism is what a lot of young writers are being greeted with, instead of any appreciation of the world of imagination in which they (the writers) have been trying, with greater or lesser success, to live . . .

In His Own Time, p. 156

8

Fitzgerald as Critic

"A classic," suggested Anthony, "is a successful book that has survived the reaction of the next period or generation. Then it's safe, like a style in architecture or furniture. It's acquired a picturesque dignity to take the place of its fashion . . ."

The Beautiful and Damned, p. 47

◆

". . . I'm not a realist," he said, and then: "No, only the romanticist preserves the things worth preserving."

The Beautiful and Damned, p. 73

◆

The play is, like most of my stuff, a very bad performance full of exceedingly good things.

to George Jean Nathan, 1922

Letters, p. 489

◆

Am undecided about *Ulysses* application to me—which is as near as I ever come to forming an impersonal judgment.

to Edmund Wilson, 1922
Letters, p. 364

◆

This is to tell you about a young man named Ernest Hemingway who lives in Paris (an American), writes for the *Transatlantic Review* and has a brilliant future. . . . I'd look him up right away. He's the real thing.

to Max Perkins, 1924
Letters, p. 187

◆

My new novel appears in late March: *The Great Gatsby*. It represents about a year's work and I think it's about ten years better than anything I've done. All my harsh smartness has been kept ruthlessly out of it—it's the greatest weakness in my work, distracting and disfiguring it even when it calls up an isolated sardonic laugh. I don't think this has a touch left. I wanted to call it *Trimalchio* (it's laid on Long Island) but I was voted down by Zelda and everybody else.

to Ernest Boyd, 1925
Letters, p. 497

◆

What I cut out of it [*The Great Gatsby*] both physically and emotionally would make another novel!

In His Own Time, p. 156

◆

If I knew anything I'd be the best writer in America.

to Max Perkins, 1926
Letters, p. 222

◆

I think it is obvious that my respect for your artistic life is absolutely unqualified, that save for a few of the dead or dying old men you are the only man writing fiction in America that I look up to very much. There are pieces and paragraphs of your work that I read over and over— in fact, I stopped myself doing it for a year and a half because I was afraid that your particular rhythms were going to creep in on mine by process of infiltration.

to Ernest Hemingway, 1934
Letters, p. 336

◆

. . . I read it [*In Our Time* by Ernest Hemingway] with the most breathless unwilling interest I have experienced since Conrad first bent my reluctant eyes upon the sea.

Afternoon of an Author, p. 120

◆

She had written a book about optimism called *Wake Up and Dream*, which had the beautiful rusty glow of a convenient half-truth—a book that left out illness and death, war, insanity, and all measure of achievement, with titillating comfortability. She had also written a wretched novel and a subsequent volume telling her friends how to write fiction, so she was on her way to being a prophet in the great American Tradition.

The Crack-Up, p. 178

◆

The novel of selected incidents has this to be said: that the great writer like Flaubert has consciously left out the stuff that Bill or Joe (in his case, Zola) will come along and say presently. He will say only the things that he alone sees. So *Madame Bovary* becomes eternal while Zola already rocks with age. . . .

    That, in brief, is my case against you, if it can be called that when I admire you so much and think your talent is unmatchable in this or any other country.

to Thomas Wolfe, 1937
Letters, p. 574

◆

The Marjorie Rawlings' book [*The Yearling*] fascinated me. I thought it was even better than *South Moon Under* and I envy her the ease with which she does action scenes, such as the tremendously complicated hunt sequence, which I would have to stake off in advance and which would probably turn out to be a stilted business in the end. Hers just simply flows; the characters keep their thinking, talking, feeling and don't stop, and you think and talk and feel with them.

to Max Perkins, 1938
Letters, p. 304

◆

I read it [*Gone with the Wind*]—I mean really read it—it is a good novel—not very original, in fact leaning heavily on *The Old Wives' Tale, Vanity Fair*, and all that has been written on the Civil War. There are no new characters, new techniques, new observations—none of the elements that make literature—especially no new examination into human emotions. But on the other hand it is interesting, surprisingly honest, consistent and workmanlike throughout, and I felt no contempt for it but only a certain pity for those who consider it the supreme achievement of the human mind.

to Frances Scott Fitzgerald, 1939
Letters, p. 65

◆

. . . please do not leave good books half-finished, you spoil them for yourself. You shouldn't have started *War and Peace*, which is a man's book and may interest you later. But you should finish both the Defoe and the Samuel Butler. Don't be so lavish as to ruin masterpieces for yourself. There are not enough of them!

to Frances Scott Fitzgerald, 1939
Letters, pp. 67–68

◆

Your comment on the satirical quality in English fiction is very apt. If you want a counter-irritant read *Bleak House* (Dickens' best book)—or if you want to explore the emotional world—not now, but in a few more years—read Dostoevski's *Brothers Karamazov*. And you'll see what the novel can do. Glad you like Butler—I liked the place where Ernest's father "turned away to conceal his lack of emotion." My God—what precision of hatred is in those lines. I'd like to be able to destroy my few detestations . . . with such marksmanship as that.

to Frances Scott Fitzgerald, 1939
Letters, p. 69

◆

A novel interests me on one of two counts: either it is something entirely new and fresh and profoundly felt, as, for instance, "The Red Badge of Courage" or "Salt," or else it is a tour de force by a man of exceptional talent, a Mark Twain or a Tarkington. A great book is both these things . . .

In His Own Time, p. 127

9

Publishing

Of course I want the binding [of *The Great Gatsby*] to be absolutely uniform with my other books—the stamping too—and the jacket we discussed before. This time I don't want any signed blurbs on the jacket—not Mencken's or Lewis' or Howard's [playwright Sidney Howard] or anyone's. I'm tired of being the author of *This Side of Paradise* and I want to start over.

to Max Perkins, 1924
Letters, p. 188

◆

. . . I am confused at what you say about Gertrude Stein. I thought it was one purpose of critics and publishers to educate the public up to original work. The first people who risked Conrad certainly didn't do it as a commercial venture. Did the evolution of startling work into accepted work cease twenty years ago?

to Max Perkins, 1924; *Letters*, p. 189

◆

If the book [*The Great Gatsby*] fails commercially it will be from one of two reasons or both.

First, the title is only fair, rather bad than good.

Second *and most important*, the book contains no important woman character, and women control the fiction market at present. I don't think the unhappy end matters particularly.

to Max Perkins, 1925
Letters, p. 201

◆

Suggested line for [book] jacket: "Show transition from his early exuberant stories of youth which created a new type of American girl and the later and more serious mood which produced *The Great Gatsby* and marked him as one of the half-dozen masters of English prose now writing in America. . . . What other writer has shown such unexpected developments, such versatility, changes of pace," etc., etc., etc. I think that, toned down as you see fit, is the general line. Don't say "Fitzgerald has done it!" and then in the next sentence that I am an artist. People who are interested in artists aren't interested in people who have "done it." Both are O.K. but don't belong in the same ad. This is an author's quibble. All authors have one quibble.

However, you have always done well by me (except for Black's memorable excretion in the *Alumni Weekly*, do you remember—"Make it a Fitzgerald Christmas!") and I leave it to you.

to Max Perkins on *The Great Gatsby*, 1925
Letters, p. 211

◆

I should say to be careful in saying it's my first book in seven years *not to imply that it contains seven years'* work. People would expect too much in bulk and scope. . . .

No exclamatory "At last, the long awaited, etc." That merely creates the "Oh yeah" mood in people.

to Max Perkins, 1933
Letters, p. 262

◆

Of course I think blurbs have gotten to be pretty much the bunk, but maybe that is a writer's point of view and the lay reader does not understand the back-scratching that is at the root of most of them. However, I leave it in your hands.

to Max Perkins, 1933
Letters, pp. 261–62

◆

It is not beyond the limits of imagination to suppose that this condition, in which only the choices of the

Book-of-the-Month get across big, may be a permanent condition. It is conceivable that the local bookstore, except as represented by such as yours and Brentano's, will become as obsolete as the silent picture. For one thing the chain-store buying and the job-lot-buying department stores seem to condemn the independent bookstores to the situation that they have reached in Baltimore where . . . they can only be compared to the fallow antique shops.

to Max Perkins, 1934

Letters, pp. 269–70

◆

Now, about advertising [for *Tender Is the Night*]. Again I want to tell you my theory that everybody is absolutely dead on ballyhoo of any kind . . . The reputation of a book must grow from within upward, must be a natural growth. I don't think there is a comparison between this book and *The Great Gatsby* as a seller. *The Great Gatsby* had against it its length and its purely masculine interest. This book, on the contrary, is a woman's book. I think, given a decent chance, it will make its own way insofar as fiction is selling under present conditions.

to Max Perkins, 1934

Letters, p. 273

◆

In general, as you know, I don't approve of great ballyhoo advertisements, even of much quoted praise. The
public is very, very, very weary of being sold bogus goods
and this inevitably reacts on solider manufactures.

to Max Perkins, 1934

Letters, p. 266

10

The Writing Life

The history of my life is the history of the struggle between an overwhelming urge to write and a combination of circumstances bent on keeping me from it.

When I lived in St. Paul and was about twelve I wrote all through every class in school in the back of my geography book and first year Latin and on the margins of themes and declensions and mathematics problems. Two years later a family congress decided that the only way to force me to study was to send me to boarding school. This was a mistake. It took my mind off my writing. I decided to play football, to smoke, to go to college, to do all sorts of irrelevant things that had nothing to do with the real business of life, which, of course, was the proper mixture of description and dialogue in the short story.

But in school I went off on a new tack. I saw a musical comedy called The Quaker Girl, and from that day forth my desk bulged with Gilbert & Sullivan librettos and dozens of notebooks containing the germs of dozens of musical comedies. . . .

I spent my entire Freshman year [at Princeton] writing an operetta for the Triangle Club. To do this I failed in algebra, trigonometry, coördinate geometry and hygiene. But the Triangle Club accepted my show, and by tutoring all through a stuffy August I managed to come back a Sophomore . . .

The next year, 1916–17, found me back in college, but by this time I had decided that poetry was the only thing worth while, so with my head ringing with the meters of Swinburne and the matters of Rupert Brooke I spent the spring doing sonnets, ballads and rondels into the small hours. I had read somewhere that every great poet had written great poetry before he was twenty-one. I had only a year and, besides, war was impending. I must publish a book of startling verse before I was engulfed.

By autumn I was in an infantry officers' training camp at Fort Leavenworth, with poetry in the discard and a brand-new ambition—I was writing an immortal novel. Every evening, concealing my pad behind Small Problems for Infantry, I wrote paragraph after paragraph on a somewhat edited history of me and my imagination. . . .

Every Saturday at one o'clock when the week's work was over I hurried to the Officers' Club, and there, in a corner of a roomful of smoke, conversation and rattling newspapers, I wrote a one-hundred-and-twenty-thousand-word novel on the consecutive week-ends of three months. There was no revising; there was no time for it. As I finished each chapter I sent it to a typist in Princeton.

Meanwhile I lived in its smeary pencil pages. The drills, marches and Small Problems for Infantry were a shadowy dream. My whole heart was concentrated upon my book.

I went to my regiment happy. I had written a novel. The war could now go on. I forgot paragraphs and pentameters, similes and syllogisms. I got to be a first lieutenant, got my orders overseas—and then the publishers wrote me that though The Romantic Egotist was the most original manuscript they had received for years they couldn't publish it. It was crude and reached no conclusion.

It was six months after this that I arrived in New York . . . I became an advertising man at ninety dollars a month, writing the slogans that while away the weary hours in rural trolley cars. After hours I wrote stories—from March to June. There were nineteen altogether; the quickest written in an hour and a half, the slowest in three days. No one bought them, no one sent personal letters. I had one hundred and twenty-two rejection slips pinned in a frieze about my room. I wrote movies. I wrote song lyrics. I wrote complicated advertising schemes. I wrote poems. I wrote sketches. I wrote jokes. Near the end of June I sold one story for thirty dollars.

On the Fourth of July, utterly disgusted with myself and all the editors, I went home to St. Paul and informed family and friends that I had given up my position and had come home to write a novel. They nodded politely, changed the subject and spoke of me very gently. But this time I knew what I was doing. I had a novel to write at last, and all through two hot months I wrote and revised and compiled and boiled down. On September fifteenth This Side of Paradise was accepted by special delivery.

Afternoon of an Author, pp. 83–85

◆

In a daze I told the Scribner Company that I didn't expect my novel [*This Side of Paradise*] to sell more than twenty thousand copies and when the laughter died away I was told that a sale of five thousand was excellent for a first novel. I think it was a week after publication that it passed the twenty thousand mark, but I took myself so seriously that I didn't even think it was funny.

These weeks in the clouds ended abruptly a week later when Princeton turned on the book—not undergraduate Princeton but the black mass of faculty and alumni.

The Crack-Up, p. 88

◆

And then, suddenly, everything changed, and this article is about that first wild wind of success and the delicious mist it brings with it. It is a short and precious time—for when the mist rises in a few weeks, or a few months, one finds that the very best is over. . . .

Then the postman rang, and that day I quit work and ran along the streets, stopping automobiles to tell friends and acquaintances about it—my novel *This Side of Paradise* was accepted for publication. That week the postman rang and rang, and I paid off my terrible small debts, bought a suit, and woke up every morning with a world of ineffable toploftiness and promise.

While I waited for the novel to appear, the metamorphosis of amateur into professional began to take place—a sort of stitching together of your whole life into a pattern of work, so that the end of one job is automatically the beginning of another. I had been an amateur before; in October, when I strolled with a girl among the stones of a southern graveyard, I was a professional and my enchantment with certain things that she felt and said was already paced by an anxiety to set them down in a story . . .

The Crack-Up, p. 86

◆

I'm wild for books and none are forthcoming . . . I wrote mine [*This Side of Paradise*] (as Stevenson wrote *Treasure Island*) to satisfy my own craving for a certain type of novel.

to Shane Leslie, 1918

Letters, p. 398

•

"The Four Fists," latest of my stories to be published, was the first to be written. I wrote it in desperation one evening because I had a three-inch pile of rejection slips and it was financially necessary for me to give the magazine what they wanted. The appreciation it has received has amazed me.

to John Grier Hibben, 1920

Letters, p. 481

•

Still, as you know, I really am in this game seriously and for something besides money and . . . I'd rather live on less and preserve the one duty of a sincere writer—to set down life as he sees it as gracefully as he knows how.

to Mr. and Mrs. Philip McQuillan, 1920

Letters, p. 484

•

I don't want to talk about myself because I'll admit I did that somewhat in this book [*This Side of Paradise*]. In fact to write it, it took three months; to conceive it—three minutes; to collect the data in it—all my life. The idea of writing it came on the first of last July; it was a substitute form of dissipation.

to the Booksellers' Convention, 1920

Letters, p. 477

◆

[I] Hope Wigham [Henry James Wigham, publisher of *Metropolitan Magazine*] is back from Paris so he can pay for this new story. It's a plot that's haunted me for two years and is like nothing I've ever read before. Of course that's against it with the American public which prefers the immemorial jaw-breakers. . . . I don't believe it's possible to stand still— you've either got to go ahead or slide back and in *The Popular Girl* I was merely repeating the *matter* of an earlier period without being able to capture the exuberant *manner*. Still I hope to God that *The Popular Girl* is bought by the movies.

to Harold Ober, 1921

As Ever, Scott Fitz-, p. 34

◆

I am rather discouraged that a cheap story like *The Popular Girl* written in one week while the baby was being born brings $1500.00 + a genuinely imaginative thing into which I put three weeks real entheusiasm [*sic*] *The Diamond in the Sky* brings not a thing. But, by God + Lorimer, I'm going to make a fortune yet.

to Harold Ober, 1922

As Ever, Scott Fitz-, p. 36

◆

"You're crazy! By your own statement I should have attained some experience by trying."

"Trying what?" cried Maury fiercely. "Trying to pierce the darkness of political idealism with some wild, despairing urge toward truth? Sitting day after day supine in a rigid chair and infinitely removed from life staring at the tip of a steeple through the trees, trying to separate, definitely and for all time, the knowable from the unknowable? Trying to take a piece of actuality and give it glamor from your own soul to make for that inexpressible quality it possessed in life and lost in transit to paper or canvas? . . ."

The Beautiful and Damned, p. 256

◆

". . . I get a thing I call sentence-fever that must be like buck-fever—it's a sort of intense literary self-consciousness that comes when I try to force myself. But the really awful days aren't when I think I can't write. They're when I wonder whether any writing is worth while at all . . ."

The Beautiful and Damned, p. 188

◆

In all events I have a book of good stories for the fall. Now I shall write some cheap ones until I've accumulated enough for my next novel. When that is finished and published I'll

wait and see. If it will support me with no more intervals of
trash I'll go on as a novelist. If not, I'm going to quit, come
home, go to Hollywood and learn the movie business.

to Max Perkins, 1925
Letters, p. 201

◆

No news except I now get $2000 a story and they grow
worse and worse and my ambition is to get where I need
write no more but only novels.

to John Peale Bishop, 1925
Letters, p. 380

◆

I hate writing short stories, as you know, and only do my
six a year to have the leisure to write my novels at leisure.

to Robert Bridges of Scribners, 1926
Letters, p. 229

◆

I've seen too many others fall through the eternal trap-
door of trying to cheat the public, no matter what their
public is, with substitutes—better to let four years go by. I
wrote young and I wrote a lot and the pot takes longer to
fill up now but the novel, my novel, is a different matter
than if I'd hurriedly finished it up a year and a half ago.

to Max Perkins, 1930
Letters, p. 245

•

Ford Madox Ford once said, "Henry James was the greatest writer of his day; therefore for me the greatest man." That is all I meant by superiority. T. S. Eliot seems to me a very great person ... To me the conditions of an artistically creative life are so arduous that I can only compare to them the duties of a soldier in war-time. I simply cannot admire, say, a merchant or an educator with the intensity I reserve for other professions, and in a sense the world agrees with me. Of the Elizabethans we remember the Queen and Drake, a ruler and a captain—only *two* "people of affairs" in contrast to Bacon, Sidney, Shakespeare, Marlowe, Jonson, Raleigh. You may say that is because history is written by writers—I think it is more than that.

to Mrs. Bayard Turnbull, 1933
Letters, p. 454

•

Nobody *naturally* likes a mind quicker than their own and one more capable of getting its operation into words. It is practically something to conceal. The history of men's *minds has been the concealing of them*, until men cry out for intelligence, and the thing has to be brought into use. . . .

The mouth tight, and the teeth and lips together

are a hard thing, perhaps one of the hardest stunts in the world, but not a waste of time, because most of the great things you learn in life are in periods of enforced silence.

to Andrew Turnbull, 1933
Letters, p. 523

◆

After all, Max, I am a plodder. One time I had a talk with Ernest Hemingway, and I told him, against all the logic that was then current, that I was the tortoise and he was the hare, and that's the truth of the matter, that everything that I have ever attained has been through long and persistent struggle while it is Ernest who has a touch of genius which enables him to bring off extraordinary things with facility. I have no facility. I have a facility for being cheap, if I wanted to indulge that. . . . but when I decided to be a serious man, I tried to struggle over every point until I have made myself into a slow-moving behemoth (if that is the correct spelling), and so there I am for the rest of my life.

to Max Perkins, 1934
Letters, p. 272

◆

I throw out most of the stuff in me with delight that it is gone. That statement might be interesting to consider in relation with Ernest's [Hemingway] article in last month's *Esquire*; an unexpressed idea is often a torment, even though its expression is liable to leave an almost crazy gap in the continuity of one's thoughts.

to Max Perkins, 1934
Letters, p. 282

◆

There is no use of me trying to rush things. Even in years like '24, '28, '29, '30, all devoted to short stories, I could not turn out more than 8–9 top-price stories a year. It simply is impossible—all my stories are conceived like novels, require a special emotion, a special experience— so that my readers, if such there be, know that each time it'll be something new, not in form but in substance. (It'd be far better for me if I could do pattern stories but the pencil just goes dead on me. I wish I could think of a line of stories like the Josephine or Basil ones which could go faster and pay $3000. But no luck yet. If I ever get out of debt I want to try a second play. It's just possible I could knock them cold if I let go the vulgar side of my talent.)

to Harold Ober, 1935
Letters, p. 420

◆

The attic was the attic of Victorian fiction. It was pleasant with beams of late light slanting in on piles and piles of magazines . . . and several dozen scrap books and clipping books and photograph books and albums and "baby books" and great envelopes of un-filed items . . .

"This is the loot," the author said grimly. "This is what one has instead of a bank balance."

Afternoon of an Author, p. 188

◆

However deeply Ring [Lardner] might cut into it, his cake had exactly the diameter of Frank Chance's [baseball] diamond.

Here was his artistic problem, and it promised fu-ture trouble. So long as he wrote within that enclosure the result was magnificent: within it he heard and re-corded the voice of a continent. But when, inevitably, he outgrew his interest in it, what was Ring left with?

The Crack-Up, p. 36

◆

It was never that he [Ring Lardner] was completely sold on athletic virtuosity as the be-all and end-all of prob-lems; the trouble was that he could find nothing finer. Imagine life conceived as a business of beautiful muscu-lar organization—an arising, an effort, a good break, a sweat, a bath, a meal, a love, a sleep—imagine it achieved; then imagine trying to apply that standard to the horri-bly complicated mess of living, where nothing, even the greatest conceptions and workings and achievements, is else but messy, spotty, tortuous—and then one can imagine the confusion that Ring faced on coming out of the ball park.

The Crack-Up, p. 37

◆

It seemed a romantic business to be a successful literary man—you were not ever going to be as famous as a movie star but what note you had was probably longer-lived—you were never going to have the power of a man of strong political or religious convictions but you were certainly more independent. Of course within the practice of your trade you were forever unsatisfied—but I, for one, would not have chosen any other.

The Crack-Up, pp. 69–70

◆

I have now at last become a writer only. The man I had persistently tried to be became such a burden that I have "cut him loose" with as little compunction as a Negro lady cuts loose a rival on Saturday night. Let the good people function as such—let the overworked doctors die in harness . . . That is their contract with the gods. A writer need have no such ideals unless he makes them for himself, and this one has quit. The old dream of being an entire man in the Goethe-Byron-Shaw tradition, with an opulent American touch, a sort of combination of J. P. Morgan, Topham Beauclerk and

St. Francis of Assisi, has been relegated to the junk heap
of the shoulder pads worn for one day on the Princeton freshman football field and the overseas cap never
worn overseas.

The Crack-Up, pp. 83–84

◆

My own happiness in the past often approached such
an ecstasy that I could not share it even with the person
dearest to me but had to walk it away in quiet streets and
lanes with only fragments of it to distil into little lines in
books . . .

The Crack-Up, p. 84

◆

Books are like brothers. I am an only child. Gatsby my
imaginary eldest brother, Amory my younger, Anthony
my worry, Dick my comparatively good brother, but all
of them far from home. When I have the courage to put
the old white light on the home of my heart, then . . .

The Crack-Up, p. 176

◆

The combination of a desire for glory and an inability to
endure the monotony it entails puts many people in the
asylum. Glory comes from the unchanging din-din-din
of one supreme gift.

The Crack-Up, p. 197

◆

. . . people who really experiment with themselves find out that all the old things are true.

The Crack-Up, p. 203

◆

The play [*The Vegetable*] opened in Atlantic City in November. It was a colossal frost. People left their seats and walked out, people rustled their programs and talked audibly in bored impatient whispers. After the second act I wanted to stop the show and say it was all a mistake but the actors struggled heroically on.

Afternoon of an Author, pp. 93–94

◆

I am thirty-six years old. For eighteen years, save for a short space during the war, writing has been my chief interest in life, and I am in every sense a professional.

Yet even now when, at the recurrent cry of "Baby needs shoes," I sit down facing my sharpened pencils and block of legal-sized paper, I have a feeling of utter helplessness. I may write a story in three days or, as is more frequently the case, it may be six weeks before I have assembled anything worthy to be sent out. I can open a volume from a criminal-law library and find a thousand plots. I can go into highway and byway, parlor and kitchen, and listen to personal revelations that, at the hands of other writers, might endure forever. But all that is nothing—not even enough for a false start.

Afternoon of an Author, p. 131

◆

Once, not so long ago, when my work was hampered by so many false starts that I thought the game was up at last, and when my personal life was even more thoroughly obfuscated, I asked an old Alabama Negro:

"Uncle Bob, when things get so bad that there isn't any way out, what do you do then?" . . .

"Mr. Fitzgerald," he said, "when things get thataway I wuks."

It was good advice. Work is almost everything. But it would be nice to be able to distinguish useful work from mere labor expended. Perhaps that is part of work itself—to find the difference. Perhaps my frequent, solitary sprints around the track are profitable.

Afternoon of an Author, p. 135

◆

"Oh," said Helen Earle, polite but unimpressed. "It must be wonderful to be a writer too. It's so very interesting."

"It has its points," he said . . . he had thought for years it was a dog's life.

Afternoon of an Author, p. 199

◆

Mostly, we authors must repeat ourselves—that's the truth. We have two or three great and moving experiences in our lives—experiences so great and moving that it doesn't seem at the time that anyone else has been so caught up and pounded and dazzled and astonished and beaten and broken and rescued and illuminated and rewarded and humbled in just that way ever before.

Then we learn our trade, well or less well, and we tell our two or three stories—each time in a new disguise—maybe ten times, maybe a hundred, as long as people will listen.

Afternoon of an Author, p. 132

◆

Last summer I was hauled to the hospital with high fever and a tentative diagnosis of typhoid. My affairs were in no better shape than yours are, reader. There was a story I should have written to pay my current debts, and I was haunted by the fact that I hadn't made a will. . . . I continued to rail against my luck that just at this crucial moment I should have to waste two weeks in bed, answering the baby talk of nurses and getting nothing done at all. But three days after I was discharged I had finished a story about a hospital.

The material was soaking in and I didn't know it. I

was profoundly moved by fear, apprehension, worry, impatience; every sense was acute, and that is the best way of accumulating material for a story.

Afternoon of an Author, pp. 132–33

◆

Someday I'm going to write about the series of calamities that led up to the awful state I was in Xmas. A writer not writing is practically a maniac within himself.

to Mr. and Mrs. Eben Finney, 1937
Letters, p. 569

◆

I never blame failure—there are too many complicated situations in life—but I am absolutely merciless toward lack of effort.

to Frances Scott Fitzgerald, 1938
Letters, p. 59

◆

Nothing is more fatuous than the American habit of labeling one of their four children as the artist on a sort of family tap day as if the percentage of artists who made any kind of go of the lousy business was one to four. It's much closer to 1 to 400,000. You've got to have the egotism of a maniac with the clear triple-thinking of a Flaubert. The amount of initial talent or let us say skill and facility is a very small element in the long struggle whose most happy [end] can only be a mercifully swift exhaustion. Who'd want to live on like Kipling with a name one no longer owned—the empty shell of a gift long since accepted and consumed?

to Judge John Biggs, Jr., 1939
Letters, p. 604

◆

If I had been promoted when I was an advertising man, given enough money to marry your mother in 1920, my life might have been altogether different. I'm not sure though. People often struggle through to what they are in spite of any detours—and possibly I might have been a writer sooner or later anyhow.

to Frances Scott Fitzgerald, 1940
Letters, pp. 108–109

◆

Again let me repeat that if you start any kind of a career following the footsteps of Cole Porter and Rodgers and Hart, it might be an excellent try. Sometimes I wish I had gone along with that gang, but I guess I am too much a moralist at heart and really want to preach at people in some acceptable form rather than to entertain them.

to Frances Scott Fitzgerald, 1939
Letters, p. 79

◆

Often I think writing is a sheer paring away of oneself leaving always something thinner, barer, more meager.

to Frances Scott Fitzgerald, 1940

Letters, p. 87

◆

What little I've accomplished has been by the most laborious and uphill work, and I wish now I'd *never* relaxed or looked back—but said at the end of *The Great Gatsby*: "I've found my line—from now on this comes first. This is my immediate duty—without this I am nothing."

to Frances Scott Fitzgerald, 1940

Letters, p. 96

◆

As soon as I feel I am writing to a cheap specification my pen freezes and my talent vanishes over the hill, and I honestly don't blame them for not taking the things that I've offered to them from time to time in the past three or four years. An explanation of their new attitude is that you no longer have a chance of selling a story with an unhappy ending . . .

to Zelda Fitzgerald, 1940

Letters, pp. 136–37

◆

I expect to be back on my novel [*The Last Tycoon*] any day and this time to finish, a two months' job. The months go so fast that even *Tender Is the Night* is six years' away. I think the nine years that intervened between *The Great Gatsby* and *Tender* hurt my reputation almost beyond repair because a whole generation grew up in the meanwhile to whom I was only a writer of *Post* stories. I don't suppose anyone will be much interested in what I have to say this time and it may be the last novel I'll ever write, but it must be done now because, after fifty, one is different. One can't remember emotionally, I think, except about childhood but I have a few more things left to say.

to Zelda Fitzgerald, 1940
Letters, p. 146

◆

It's odd that my old talent for the short story vanished. It was partly that times changed, editors changed, but part of it was tied up somehow with you and me—the happy ending. Of course every third story had some other ending, but essentially I got my public with stories of young love. I must have had a powerful imagination to project it so far and so often into the past.

to Zelda Fitzgerald, 1940
Letters, p. 148

◆

I think my novel [*The Last Tycoon*] is good. I've written it with difficulty. It is completely upstream in mood and

will get a certain amount of abuse but is first hand and
I am trying a little harder than I ever have to be exact
and honest emotionally. I honestly hoped somebody else
would write it but nobody seems to be going to.

to Edmund Wilson, 1940
Letters, p. 375

◆

The present writer has always been a "natural" for his
profession, in so much that he can think of nothing he
could have done as efficiently as to have lived deeply in
the world of imagination.

In His Own Time, p. 157

◆

I told him the number of people who had turned down
my own stuff when I was young, but that never had anyone refused to read it . . .

to Mr. and Mrs. Eben Finney, 1938
Letters, p. 597

◆

". . . the whole equipment of my life is to be a novelist. And that is attained with tremendous struggle;
that is attained with a tremendous nervous struggle;
that is attained with a tremendous sacrifice which you
make to lead any profession. It was done because I was
equipped for it. I was equipped for it as a little boy. I

began at ten, when I wrote my first story. My whole life is a professional move towards that.

"Now the difference between the professional and the amateur is something that is awfully hard to analyze, it is awfully intangible. It just simply means the keen equipment; it means a scent, a smell of the future in one line." . . .

". . . To have something to say is a question of sleepless nights and worry and endless motivation of a subject, and the endless trying to dig out the essential truth, the essential justice."

Zelda, pp. 272–73

◆

"No one felt like this before—says the young writer—but *I* felt like this; I have a pride akin to a soldier going into battle; without knowing whether there will be anybody there, to distribute medals or even to record it."

But remember, also, young man: you are not the first person who has ever been alone and alone.

In His Own Time, p. 157

ACKNOWLEDGMENTS

A special thanks to Frances Scott Fitzgerald Smith and Miss Sheilah Graham for their cooperation and important contribution to F. *Scott Fitzgerald on Writing*. Grateful acknowledgment is also due to Charles Scribner III, Laurie Schieffelin, and Dennis Graham Combs for their invaluable assistance in the preparation of this book.

SOURCE CREDITS

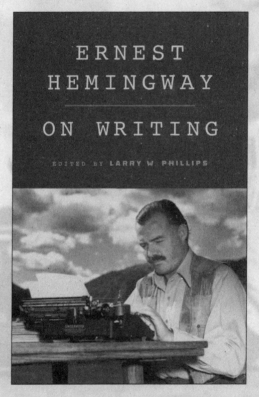